Fun with English

Good Grammar

WILLIAM EDMONDS

KINGFISHER

The author wishes to express his particular
gratitude to Robert Wheeler, the designer of all the
books in this series. There has been an especially
close collaboration at every stage and the author
has found this an immense stimulus and
encouragement. The author would also like to
thank Terry McKenna for his superbly amusing
illustrations, invaluable ingredients of the series.
The author wishes to thank Dr Trevor Pateman of
the University of Sussex for his valuable
suggestions and advice both in the planning and
revising of the text.

KINGFISHER
Kingfisher Publications Plc
New Penderel House, 283–288 High Holborn,
London WC1V 7HZ

The material in this edition was previously published
by Kingfisher Publications Plc in the *Wordmaster* series
(1993) and in the *Guide to Good English* series (1989)

This edition published by Kingfisher Publications Plc 1999
10 9 8 7 6 5 4 3 2 1
2WEB(1TR)/0100/EDK/(ATL)/140EDI

A CIP catalogue record for this book is available from
the British Library

ISBN 0 7534 0368 4

Printed in Spain

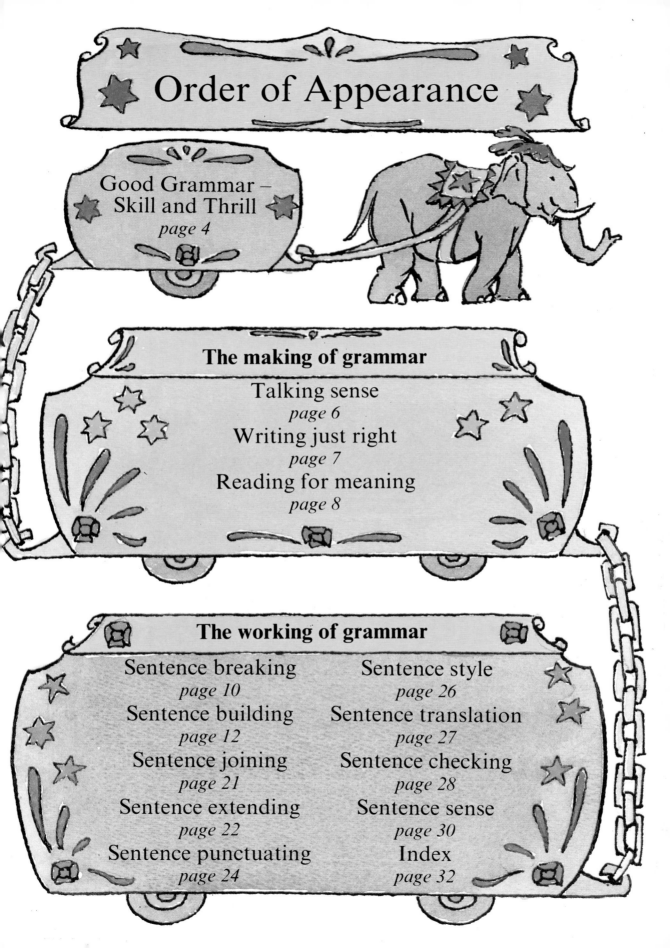

Order of Appearance

Good Grammar – Skill and Thrill

can I juggle words so that they make sen...

words up jumbled difficult to understand and
are read
you see do what mean we

(Jumbled-up words are difficult to read and understand. Do you see what we mean?)

That is why we have grammar – a way of arranging words into sentences so that they make sense for everybody.

We all love good grammar. Saying things the right way makes for funny jokes, fascinating gossip, pleasant conversations, exciting stories, interesting information, lively arguments, special secrets, enjoyable entertainment and all kinds of fun with words. Like juggling, grammar can be exciting and skilful. We can use it to make words do almost anything we like.

Learning good grammar

Learning the skills of good grammar is much easier than most of us realize. It happens in two main ways.

1 Making our own Grammar

We find ourselves making grammar all the time that we try to talk, read or write. We do it quite naturally and without first learning any rules. We want to make sense for ourselves and to fit in with the language we hear and see around us. We do this almost automatically.

2 Looking at how Grammar Works

This means looking at how sentences really work. It means breaking them apart and building them up so as to see how different kinds of words do different jobs. It means seeing how different parts of sentences fit together, and how different kinds of punctuation marks are used. It means knowing what to check for so that the sentences sound right and make complete sense.

In this book we look at both the making and working of grammar in a number of different ways. You can try and find out which of the ways helps you the most.

> Beware! This book is full of smart stuff. A little good grammar goes a long way. Once you have gained the skill it will stay with you for ever.

The making of grammar

Talking sense

From the moment we begin to talk we are learning grammar. We don't just copy somebody else's sentences like a parrot, we find ourselves inventing new ways of putting words together. What is more, most of what we say makes good sense or shows that we are learning fast.

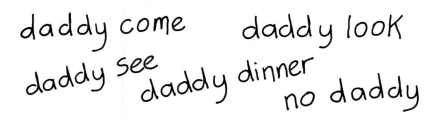

daddy come   daddy look
daddy see   daddy dinner
                  no daddy

In this way we start by making our own little sentences. As we want to say more and more so also do our sentences grow. Many of these first sentences are not quite like adult sentences or what we consider to be 'correct grammar', but they show an amazing natural skill for sentence-making and for making sense.

Just as we all want to talk, we also find ourselves all wanting to learn grammar, without realizing what we are doing. We do it because we want to make sense of our surroundings and to feel close to the people around us.

So, speaking clearly is the first and the most important way of learning grammar. Skilled talkers, such as lawyers, politicians and teachers have an especially good grounding in grammar.

Is talking good for us or just a waste of time? What do you think? Chat about this with a friend.

Speak clearly

Writing just right

Setting out to write is the second most obvious way of learning the skills of grammar.

Good writing and good grammar go hand in hand. Just as understanding grammar helps us with our writing, so also does trying to write help us to know about grammar. Nobody starts learning rules before they begin writing; if we had to do that we would never ever begin. We first try writing because we want to. There are many good reasons for doing this:

We like imitating grown-ups
We like sending messages
We like labelling
We like making up stories
We like making someone else laugh,
feel happy, frightened or sad
We like being authors

Having a good reason for writing helps us to write clearly and to use good grammar. In the Kingfisher Guide to **Good Writing** you can learn more about the many different reasons for writing.

It is funny to think that at the same time as we are *learning to write* we are also *writing to learn* grammar and many other things. So, keep on writing; it will keep on teaching you.

7

Reading for meaning

With our own talking and writing we try out and learn grammar skills for the first time. When we start reading we begin to *see* what these skills are all about.

The Iron Man came to the top of the cliff.

How far had he walked? Nobody knows. Where had he come from? Nobody knows. How was he made? Nobody knows.

Taller than a house, the Iron Man stood at the top of the cliff, on the very brink, in the darkness.

The wind sang through his iron fingers. His great iron head, shaped like a dustbin but as big as a bedroom, slowly turned to the right, slowly turned to the left. His iron ears turned, this way, that way. He was hearing the sea. His eyes, like headlamps, glowed white, then red, then infra-red, searching the sea. Never before had the Iron Man seen the sea.

He swayed in the strong wind that pressed against his back. He swayed forward, on the brink of the high cliff.

And his right foot, his enormous iron right foot, lifted — up, out, into space, and the Iron Man stepped forward, off the cliff, into nothingness.

CRRRAAAASSSSSSH!

(Reprinted by permission of Faber and Faber, Ltd. from *The Iron Man* by Ted Hughes)

The author of these words, Ted Hughes, has used grammar skills to write this story so that it is easy and

exciting to read. Supposing he had not bothered to do this:

the iron man came to the top of the cliff how far had he walked nobody knows where had he come from nobody knows how was he made nobody knows taller than . . .

If we didn't already know the story, this would be very hard to follow and to understand. But Ted Hughes arranges his words into sentences. In fact, he makes many kinds of sentences. Some of them report action. Some of them ask questions. Some of them give answers. Some of them add unusual descriptions. Some of them exclaim.

The sentences are also grouped together into several sections or paragraphs. All together, the words are skilfully arranged so that they draw you into the story and then make you want to know what is going to happen next. What is more, the spaces and other marks on the paper fit with the pauses that we find we make as we tell the story.

We are drawn into stories like this because of the good grammar. This grammar is used so well that most of the time we don't realize the trouble that has been taken in using it. By reading good examples like this we are also giving ourselves good grammar lessons.

The Iron Man

The working of grammar

Looking at the working of grammar is rather like looking at how a complicated machine works. It works only because it is fitted together in exactly the right way. In this part of the book we are going to look at how the basic machinery of English grammar is made up and how it can best be kept in good working order.

Sentence breaking

Looking at sentences and breaking them up into parts is a good way of beginning to see how they work.

The first and easiest way of breaking sentences is to look for:

subjects	and predicates
The cow	jumped over the moon.
Humpty Dumpty	had a great fall.
Jack and Jill	fell down the hill.
The Iron Man	came to the top of the hill.
The big bad wolf	tried to trick the pig.

The **subject** is who or what the sentence is first about. It is often at the beginning of a sentence, but not always. The **predicate** is what is said or written about the subject.

10

Now try and break up these sentences into subjects and predicates. (Underline the subjects.)

The sun was shining. The sky was blue. Everybody was out enjoying themselves on this lovely day. Then all of a sudden disaster struck. The ice-cream van blew up in a cloud of smoke and was never seen again. (*Answers on page 32.*)

We can already see that the predicate can be quite long and that it too can be broken into different parts.

A slightly more complicated way of breaking down many sentences is to look for:

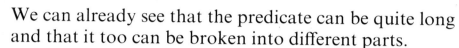

subjects	verbs	and objects
The wolf	chased	the pig.
The cat	smelled	a rat.
The cat	stayed	on the mat.
The Iron Man	came	to the top of the cliff.

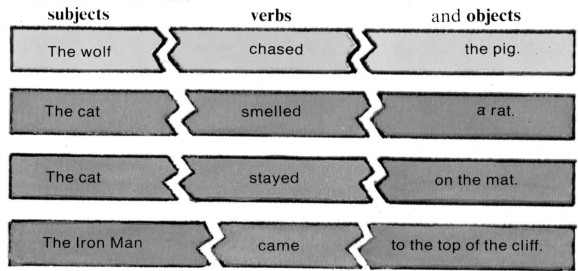

In the first two sentences the object is simple: we say they are direct objects.

In the last two sentences the objects need extra words (prepositions): so we call them indirect objects. As we shall see (*page 22*) these can also be referred to as adverbial phrases.

But most sentences are more complicated than these simple examples. They can also be broken into parts, clauses, phrases and parts of speech. We shall now find out about the different ways of building, joining and extending sentences.

subject ⟩ ⟨ verb

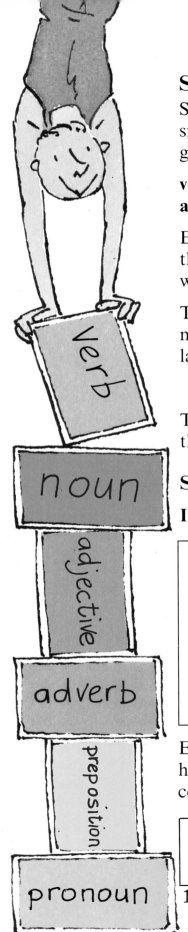

Sentence building

Sentence building is easy. We do it by making use of a small selection of building materials. These are what are generally known as *parts of speech*. Here they are:

verbs, nouns, adjectives, adverbs, prepositions, pronouns, articles, conjunctions and interjections.

Every word that we know belongs to at least one of these parts. There are also many words, as we shall see, which can belong to more than just one part.

To make it a little easier to deal with these building materials in this section we shall give them abbreviated labels:

V. N. Adj. Adv. Prep. Pro. Art. Conj. Int.

The parts of speech are also introduced and described in the Kingfisher Guide to **Good Words**.

Single word sentences

Interjections (Int.)

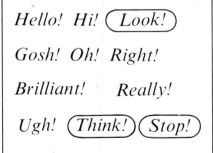

Hello! Hi! (Look!)

Gosh! Oh! Right!

Brilliant!   Really!

Ugh! (Think!)(Stop!)

 Interjections are special because they can be sentences all on their own.

Each of the particular interjections ringed above, happens also to be a verb. They are verbs used as commands (known also as *imperatives*).

See!
See how many one word orders you can make to your friend!

Two word sentences

By adding adverbs we can turn commands or exclamations into two word sentences.

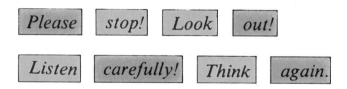

Please   stop!   Look   out!

Listen   carefully!   Think   again.

By adding certain pronouns to the verb parts we can make other two part sentences which take note of the commands.

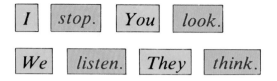

I   stop.   You   look.

We   listen.   They   think.

As we try to make two word sentences we quickly find ourselves wanting to use extra words or wanting to adapt words.

John stops immediately. He looks everywhere. We listen carefully to him. He and his friend think again.

The Key Part

In all these very short sentences one particular building part always appears. Can you see what it is?

It's the verb – the part that shows what is happening in every sentence.

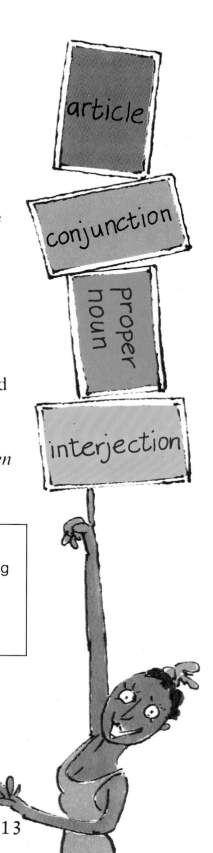

article

conjunction

proper noun

interjection

13

Building simple sentences

Articles (Art.)

a *an* *the*

any *some*

Defining or introducing words – used to point out 'which'.

Nouns (N.)

cat *dog* *boy* *elephant*

girl *mat* *house*

mouse *car* *hat* *snow*

Naming words – words that tell who or what the sentence is about.

Pronouns (Pro.)

he *she* *it* *you* *him*

her *they* *them* *me*

Words that can take the place of nouns.

Verbs (V.)

was *saw* *sat* *fell* *ran*

took *ate* *chased*

kissed *missed*

The key parts to every sentence: 'doing' or 'being' words.

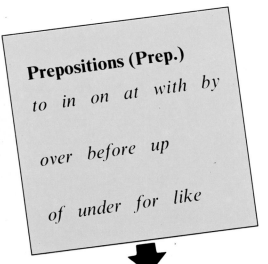

Prepositions (Prep.)

to in on at with by

over before up

of under for like

Words that introduce others, often to indicate position or, maybe, likeness.

More Nouns (N.)

Proper nouns:
Scotland   January

Wednesday

John   Ann   London

Plural nouns:
animals   children   people

houses   mice

See how many sentences you can make using the words belonging to these parts! Can you also name the parts (in abbreviation) under each word.

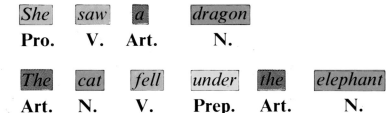

She	*saw*	*a*	*dragon*
Pro.	**V.**	**Art.**	**N.**

The	*cat*	*fell*	*under*	*the*	*elephant*
Art.	**N.**	**V.**	**Prep.**	**Art.**	**N.**

Do you find that you keep making the same kinds of sentences with the same arrangements of parts? Can you make other sentences which keep to these patterns?

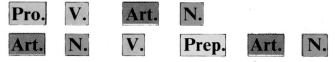

Pro. V. Art. N.

Art. N. V. Prep. Art. N.

Adding adjectives

wonderful rich mysterious little huge young old wise dirty beautiful grand tiny blue steep high green seven six two tumbled-down thatched red broken smart odd pretty wintry dark moonlit horrible surprising delightful fantastic terrifying interesting long happy

Adjectives tell us more about nouns and sometimes pronouns.

Which of these adjectives would you fit into this story. Perhaps you could even think of some others that might fit in.

Once upon a time there lived a _____ man. He lived in a _____ house on the top of a _____ hill. The house had _____ windows a _____ roof and a _____ door. It was an extremely _____ house.

One _____ night, the _____, _____ man heard a _____ noise. He couldn't think what it was. He got out of his _____ bed. He crept downstairs and opened the door to see the most _____, _____ sight that he had ever seen. He couldn't believe his eyes.

"This is _____", he said. "This is the most _____ thing that has happened to me in the whole of my _____ life.

If we use more than one adjective with a single noun we use a comma between each one.

Other kinds of adjectives

Interrogative adjectives: *Which* book . . . ?
Demonstrative adjectives: *This* book, *that* book, *these* books and *those* books.
Possessive adjectives: *my your his her their*.

The cat . . . *This* cat . . . *My* cat . . .

(Can you see how possessive adjectives and demonstrative adjectives can take the place of articles? We can say that articles are really a weak kind of adjective)

Adding adverbs

> *slowly carefully generally particularly very quite fast intently thoughtfully suspiciously just faintly gently suddenly again always never bitterly not*

Adverbs are words which are often added into sentences next to verbs. We use them to say *more* about a verb. We can also use them to tell us more about adjectives (*very* good or *disgustingly* bad) and other adverbs (*very badly* or *extremely well*).

Which of these adverbs would fit into this story?

The cat got up _____ from the mat. She looked _____ around the room. She listened _____ _____ for any suspicious noises. She sniffed the air _____ for any suspicious smells. She crept _____ to the corner of the room. She thought she could _____ smell a rat. _____ she sprang over the television and pounced. Miaow! Out she came with a _____ smelly, old shoe in her mouth. She was _____ disappointed. She was determined _____ to be fooled _____.

17

Adapting Verbs

Verbs can play amazing tricks. Any verb can be adapted into many different forms to make a sentence completely change its meaning.

As well as saying 'The acrobat balances skilfully on a tightrope', we could say 'She balanced',

'She is balancing'

'She was balancing'

'She has balanced'

'She will balance'

'She will have balanced'

'She would have balanced'

'She may balance'

'She would balance'

'She could balance'

'She may have balanced'

'She could have balanced'

'She should have balanced'

'She should balance'

18

The balancing depends on all kinds of times and conditions – or what we call the different tenses of the verb *balance*. Most of these different tenses depend on using extra verbs – auxiliary verbs. Each of them gives a distinctly different meaning to the sentences. If we add the negative adverb *not* another whole set of meanings arise just as happens if we turn them into questions (She could not balance. Does she balance? etc.).

Jumping through hoops

The lion jumps through the hoop.

> Can you adapt the verb *jump* to show its many different aspects?

Making verbs agree
Verbs are also good at changing themselves to suit their subjects. For instance, when we are writing we say:

I sit	you sit	he sits	we sit	they sit
I am	you are	he is	we are	they are
I have	you have	he has	we have	they have
I was	you were	he was	we were	they were

The dog *eats* biscuits.   The cat *bites*.

Dogs *eat* biscuits.   Some cats *bite*.

We know how to make verbs agree by having a good eye and ear for language we see and hear around us.

19

Playing about with parts

The great thing to remember about fitting parts of speech together is that many words can act in more than one part. They can be like circus performers who can do a variety of tricks.

For instance, a good few words can double up as nouns and adjectives.

We can say that *pink* (N.) is a pretty colour but also that the umbrella is *pink* (Adj.).
We can talk about *umbrellas* (N.) or about an *umbrella* (Adj.) shape.

A good few words can double up as verbs and nouns.

We can have a *fight* (N.) or we can *fight* (V.).
We can say that he went *fishing* (V.) and that the *fishing* (N.) was a success.

Some words can also act as both adverbs and adjectives, or as both prepositions and adverbs.

The car went *fast* (Adv.) because it was a *fast* (Adj.) car. It sped *away* (Adv.); *away over* (Prep.) the hill it sped.

We also have many special tricks for changing parts, especially by adding suffixes (. . . ness, . . . ful, . . . ly, etc.) as we see in the Guide to **Good Words**.

A Fight (N.)

They are
Fighting (V.)

So you see! Simple sentence building is easy. All we have to do is to choose the right parts, adapt them and change them around, if necessary, and then place them together to make sense.

Sentence joining

Conjunctions
and or but yet

Conjunctions are words which join other words together or sentences together.

Can you decide which conjunction is best for each joining space?

The elephants led the parade _____ were followed by the horses. All the animals performed beautifully _____ the clowns behaved very badly. They threw water at the audience _____ covered themselves in custard pies. We could not decide whether we liked the acrobats best _____ whether we preferred the jugglers.

If we only speak or write in short simple sentences our language quickly becomes jerky and uncomfortable. So we often use conjunctions to join up sentences.

Conjunctions in pairs

either . . . or   neither . . . nor
not only . . . but also
both . . . and

but...

Subordinating conjunctions

like before when
if because . . .

Words which introduce extra clauses into sentences. We shall look at these in the next section.

21

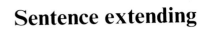

Sentence extending

The clown fell over.

The clown with the funny face fell

The clown whose face was brightly painted fell into the

Extending sentences means making them longer and more interesting. Instead of thinking just of individual words we can begin to think of different groups within a sentence. These groups can also act like single parts of speech. We call these extensions phrases and clauses.

Phrases
A phrase is a group of words which does not make complete sense on its own. It has no verb.

Adjectival phrases act as extended adjectives, adding descriptions.

The cat *with the white spot* caught a rat.
The girl *sitting at the back* was talking.

Adverbial phrases act as extended adverbs, answering the questions How? When? Why? and Where? about the verb.

The cat caught the rat *in the barn.*
The girl was talking *all the time.*

Noun phrases act as nouns.

Both the cat and the girl were friends.
A phrase is *a group of words without a verb.*

into a bucket of water.

water because he was tripped up.

Clauses

A clause is a group of words with a verb. Sentences often contain more than one clause, a main clause and a subordinate clause or two.

She began talking   *when she was one.*

He ate two pies   *because he was so hungry.*

These are main   These are subordinate or
clauses   secondary clauses

The subordinate clauses in this case also happen to be adverbial clauses, adding to the verb in the main clause.

Adjectival clauses often begin with *who, which, that, whose* or *whom.*

The boy *who was always eating pies* was very fat.
The girl *whom I saw in the road* was an amazing sight.

Noun clauses act as nouns.

I saw *what she was doing.*
We knew *that he was eating.*

Build your own extensions!
See how many different ways you can extend these simple sentences with phrases and clauses: *The mouse climbed onto the giant. The princess met a frog.*

Sentence punctuating

Punctuating means making points. It means putting the right kind of points in just the right place so as to point out the length, shape and exact meaning of sentences.

$\boxed{.}$ $\boxed{?}$ $\boxed{!}$ **Full stops, question marks** and **exclamation marks** all point out sentence endings.

Full stops are at the end of sentences that are statements. Question marks indicate questions. Don't they?

Look out! Please use !!! for orders and exclamations!

These are the most important markers for every sentence.

Stops also have extra uses.
If part of a sentence is missing . . .
A short row of stops also has its uses, as you see.
Also, a single stop can be used for shortening some titles or names. *Sun. 14th Feb. J. Smith*

$\boxed{,}$ **Commas** point out brief pauses in a sentence.

● They can help, for instance, to distinguish the different sections of extended longer sentences, which we talked about on the previous page.

● They are useful when we make lists of words, or have a list of succeeding main clauses.

There were elephants, lions, kangaroos and penguins. The elephants stood still, the lions growled, the kangaroos hopped away and the penguins just flapped around.

Notice how we don't usually put a comma before the conjunction *and*!

| " | " | **"Inverted commas** are used to show words that are directly spoken", said the teacher. She added, "They are also called speech marks because they are put at both the beginning and the end of the words actually spoken".

| 's | **Apostrophes** by the letter *s* indicate belonging.

John's bike   Jane's speedboat

We have to be careful when the belonger word also ends in *s* like *boys*: we then say *the boys' bikes*.

Apostrophes are also used to show missing letters in shortened words or shortened combined words:

3 o'clock (of the) don't can't they're we'll (we will or shall)

| : | **Colons** can be used before a list of items like this: jam; sugar; cheese; biscuits; bread and butter.
| ; | We can use **semi-colons** to separate each item or we could also use commas in this case. Semi-colons can also be used as a stronger natural break in a longer sentence; otherwise we might use a conjunction.

| - | **Hyphens** are used to join two words which are linked together like *seat-belts jelly-babies* and so on. A set of two hyphens - indicating an extra comment - can also be used in the middle of sentences in the same way as brackets ( ) are used.

<u>**Underlining**</u> a word gives it special emphasis.

She <u>was</u> sitting on his hat. (but not anymore)

She was sitting on <u>his</u> hat. (not anyone else's)

She was sitting on his <u>hat</u>. (not his gloves)

Sentence style

Style is the personal touch which makes sentences look and sound appealing. The working of grammar needs style every bit as much as it needs the correct fitting together of parts, phrases and clauses.

Here are a few tips about style:

Vary the length of sentences.
To make sentences follow each other comfortably it helps to make them of different lengths. Some may be short. Others may be longer with clauses and sub clauses which make them more complicated.

Vary the building patterns of sentences.
Try and start the sentences in different ways.

Avoid repetition of important words or phrases.
Using pronouns instead of nouns can often help. It is also helpful to find synonyms (different words with similar meanings such as *difficult* and *hard*).

Remember who you are writing for.
Try to keep their interest.

Use words which sound good together.
Enjoy the thrills and skills of good grammar!
Strive for style!
This is what poets do especially. It is always good to have an ear for the sound patterns of words as well as an eye for the way words look together.

Remember, lastly, who you are or the sort of person you wish your readers to think you are.
It's your personal style which shapes your writing.

Sentence translation

Learning another language can teach us a lot about the working of our own grammar.

Many of the ways we use to look at English grammar come from the study of Latin, the language of the Ancient Romans. Latin grammar follows its own rules, using fewer words than English.

LATIN

Feles nigra in stoream sedebat

cat   black on mat   was sitting

ENGLISH

The black cat was sitting on the mat.

FRENCH

Le chat noir s'   était assis   sur le   tapis.

The cat   black itself was   seated on the mat.

In French it takes 9 words to say the same thing, as opposed to 5 in Latin and 8 in English.

URDU

رستّی ٹالیں پر کالی بلّ تھی پہ بیٹھ

     mat   cat   black   Is   sat   on

In Urdu the sentence is made up from right to left with 6 words.

Each of these four languages (English, Latin, French and Urdu) uses different numbers of words, different kinds of words and different word arrangements in order to make the same meaning. They each have their own special grammars.

So you see, grammars are keys for unlocking languages. That is why they are so useful.

27

Sentence checking

All good writers like to check their sentences after they have finished
their writing. They want to be sure that the grammar is working well.
It often helps to have the help of another reader such as a friend, a
teacher or editor – someone who is a trained expert at such work.
Here are some of the questions writers and editors ask themselves
when checking sentences:

1 | Do all the sentences begin and end correctly? | Make sure the first word of each sentence has a capital letter and that the sentence ends with a full-stop, a question mark or an exclamation mark.

G ~~g~~ood grammar needs careful attention.

2 | Do all the sentences have a verb? |

are
Verbs ∧ absolutely essential for all
proper sentences.

3 | Are the sentences too long? | Look out for sentences that go on and on, leaving you breathless and confused! As a general rule it is advisable not to use more than one single conjunction (*and or but*) in any sentence.

The boy ran down the road₀ ~~and~~ *H*e went
round the corner and ~~then~~ he saw an
elephant₀ ~~and~~ *H*e went for a ride. and all
his friends waved.

4 | Are nouns and pronouns used wisely? | Good writers try to avoid repeating the same
nouns because *they* ~~good writers~~ know how useful
pronouns can be. They also know that ~~they~~ *Pronouns*
should only be used when who or what is
being referred to is unmistakable.

28

Re-read and check

Are there any other possible double meanings?

5 Be careful about the placing of extra phrases or clauses!

The fire was put out before any damage was done by the fire brigade.

Are all the natural pauses (and asides) correctly punctuated?

6

Remember, punctuation pays off. Doesn't it?

Do the verbs keep to the same tense?

7 Stories can be told in a present tense or in a past tense. It does not make sense to change tense.

The clowns enter. They fall over each other.
                                                    run
They throw custard pies and they ~~ran~~ away.

Are there any 'split infinitives'?

8 'Infinitives' are verbs in their basic form with the word *to* in front of them like *to be, to put* or *to read.*

It is easy to carelessly put adverbs in the middle of infinitives. Split infinitives are usually rather clumsy to comfortably read.

Is the writing up to *Standard*?

9 Avoid using slang or language which is generally not understood or accepted by everybody. We expect writing to be more polished than the language of ordinary talking. This is what we call *Standard English*.

Does each sentence really make sense? **10**

Sentence Sense

Welcome to the circus!
Learn the skills!
Enjoy the thrills!
It all makes sense
with sentences.

Index

Answers to page 11
The subjects are "The sun", "The sky", "Everybody", "disaster" and "The ice-cream van". All the other words make up the predicates.